FREE FROM PAIN SERIES
HELP FOR HIP PAIN

Dr George Ampat
Consultant Orthopaedic Surgeon
*Minimise medication, scale down surgeries
and exercise enthusiastically*

DISCLAIMER

This book is intended to provide general educational information only and is not meant to substitute for professional medical advice. Each patient and condition is unique, so solutions, treatments, and results vary. Please use the information in this book alongside the advice from your regular doctor.

Copyright © 2024 George Ampat All rights reserved. No part of this publication may be reproduced, distributed, or transmitted in any form or by any means, including photocopying, recording or other electronic or mechanical methods without prior written permission.

Talita Cumi Ltd 681, Liverpool Road, Southport PR8 3NS
www.ampat.co.uk
www.freefrompain.org.uk

Printed in the United Kingdom
Ampat, George
Help for Hip Pain
ISBN 978-0-9956769-7-8

Special thanks to Dr Sarah Bazin OBE for writing the foreword to this book.

To Dr Jemima George and Daisy Pagonis who contributed to editing the book.

To all my patients over the years who have taught me so much.

To Susan, Talita and Jemima for your constant inspiration, support and love.

Foreword

I was delighted to be invited by Dr. Ampat to write the foreword for his book **Help for Hip Pain**. As a Chartered Physiotherapist, I have dedicated my career to encouraging people to stay active and keep moving, even when faced with pain and reduced mobility.

This book is aimed at individuals experiencing a loss of function that limits their ability to fully engage in life. It offers both understanding and practical solutions.

The first part of the book clearly explains, with the help of detailed diagrams, the science behind joint changes and the resulting pain and stiffness. This foundational knowledge is essential for understanding the causes of these physical changes and sets the stage for the rationale behind the exercise programme that follows.

The ARISE plan introduces a graded approach to exercise, emphasising the importance of beginning within one's current capabilities and progressing only after mastering each level — a true training programme in every sense.

The final section outlines 12 exercises that form the ARISE plan, complete with guidance on progression. These exercises are designed to be achievable, structured, and empowering.

This book is a much-needed resource. I am confident that those living with arthritic changes will find its clear explanations and practical guidance to be of great value.

Sarah Bazin
OBE FCSP
March 2025

HIP PAIN INTRODUCTION – a word from the author

Hip pain can be a debilitating condition, restricting your ability to mobilise and engage with loved ones and can negatively impact your quality of life. It reduces the amount you can truly experience life to the fullest and can affect your mood and happiness.

It can be hard to know what to do in these situations, and with a lot of conflicting advice and evidence out there, it can feel like trudging through muddy waters.

These two factors inspired me to write this book. This book finally puts you back in the driving seat, empowering you to take back control over your body and start on the path to restoring your life to the full. Through this book, I aim to educate you, the reader, about the causes of hip pain and a little about the basic science behind it. Then, I will guide you through evidence-based guidance on treatment options. Through the methods in this book, I want you to feel aware of the changes you can make to facilitate a life not restricted by pain.

This book will follow the following structure:

Part One – The cause of your pain and the science behind it
Part Two – The evidence-based arguments for exercising your pain away
Part Three – The ARISE plan - an exercise programme designed for you
Part Four – The 12 exercises that form part of the ARISE plan

All the exercises can be viewed at https://youtu.be/cqo1ELc1lNc
In addition, beside each exercise, there is a QR code. Your smartphone camera should take you to that particular exercise on the net.

  Scan this QR Code on your phone to view all the exercises on Youtube.

Part 1

The cause of your pain and the science behind it

What is arthritis?

Our bodies are made of skin, fat, muscle, bones, and other organs. The skin serves as a covering. The fat provides insulation and padding and is also a store of energy. The muscle gives us the strength to stand and move. The bones contribute to our structure and shape. The other organs have various functions to sustain a healthy life.

Our bones are connected through separate joints. The ends of our bones are covered with smooth, shiny cartilage, which allows our joints to move smoothly. Arthritis occurs when these joints become damaged, causing inflammation, pain, and stiffness. Arthritis is the most common cause of hip pain.

HEALTHY HIP JOINT

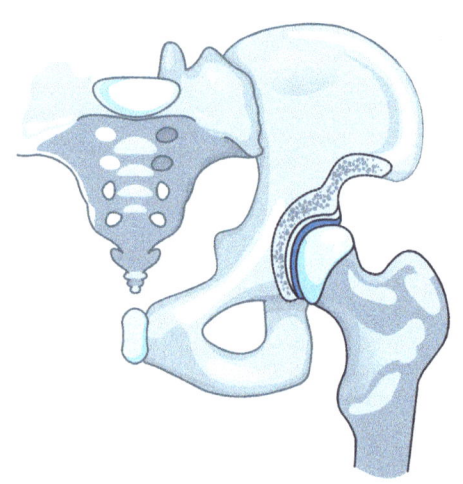

OSTEOARTHRITIS IS AGE RELATED

INFLAMMATORY ARTHRITIS IS IMMUNE RELATED

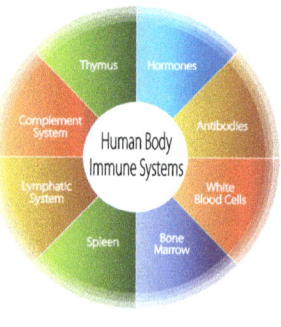

Types of arthritis

There are mainly two types of arthritis: osteoarthritis and inflammatory arthritis. Osteoarthritis is very common and is an age-related change. As one becomes old, the joints become slightly arthritic. For some, this age-related change does not cause pain, but it can cause some discomfort for others.

Inflammatory arthritis is less common than osteoarthritis and is seen in certain conditions such as rheumatoid arthritis, ankylosing spondylitis, and psoriatic arthritis.

Osteoarthritis

Osteoarthritis is commonly referred to as "wear and tear arthritis." In osteoarthritis, the cartilage structure changes, becoming harder and less flexible. The thickness of the cartilage also reduces. "Wear and tear" is no longer considered the correct description for osteoarthritis. It is now referred to as "wear and repair" arthritis. We will explain the need for this change in the following page.

There are no medicines to control osteoarthritis, and current medications only control the pain for a limited time. Exercise and diet are the only methods to help with osteoarthritis.

HIP OSTEOARTHRITIS

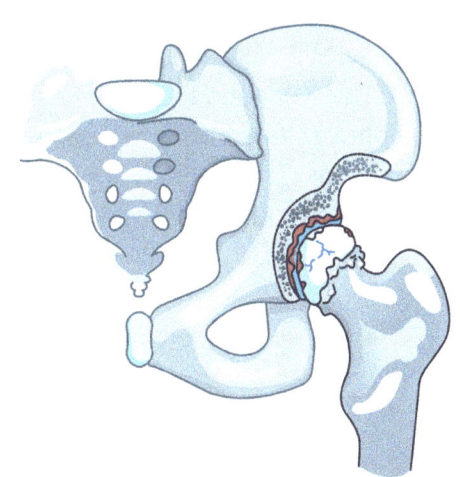

WARRIOR CELLS ATTACKING THE JOINT IN INFLAMMATORY ARTHRITIS

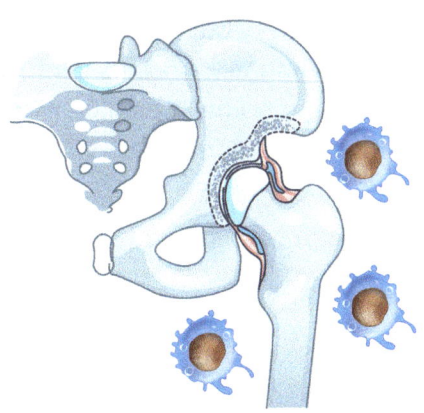

Inflammatory arthritis

In inflammatory arthritis, the warrior cells of the immune system, which are meant to fight the bugs that enter our bodies, may become defective and start attacking our joints. This leads to the destruction of the joint.

Luckily, with advancements in medical research, medications are available that can suppress the activity of these immune system warrior cells and prevent them from attacking our joints.

"Wear and tear"

Although osteoarthritis is commonly referred to as "wear and tear arthritis," it is not really a result of normal daily use. We will use an example to illustrate this. The wear and tear we are subjected to inside the body differs from the wear and tear we see in our shoes. The older and more used the shoe, the more worn out it becomes.

THE OLDER AND MORE USED THE SHOE THE MORE WORN IT WOULD BE

NEW SHOE   OLD AND USED SHOE

NORMAL USE DOES NOT CAUSE OSTEOARTHRITIS

"Wear and repair"

This is not the case with osteoarthritis. There is no evidence that regular day-to-day use of our joints will cause osteoarthritis. As we use our joints, the cells are not worn away but are renewed constantly. "Wear and tear" occurs in objects that do not have life. Our bodies have life, meaning our joints go through wear and repair.

If normal day-to-day use does not cause osteoarthritis, then what does?

The overuse or underuse of our joints can cause osteoarthritis.

Overuse causes osteoarthritis

Walking and running, as our forefathers did, will not cause osteoarthritis. However, extremely excessive movements like running ultramarathons, extreme sports and very heavy weightlifting can put too much strain on our joints. This is because these activities exceed the ability of our joints to repair themselves.

However, normal physical activity will not cause osteoarthritis. Regular exercise, such as walking, running, jogging, swimming, and cycling, can protect against it.

Underuse causes osteoarthritis

This type of wear occurs when the muscles are weak. Sedentariness or inactivity usually results in weak muscles.

If the muscles are weak, there is an increased risk of the joint wearing out. This is because the lack of muscle strength causes the joint to wobble when used. This instability causes friction and strain across the joint surface.

Stronger muscles will stabilise the joint and allow the joints to glide smoothly without any wobble.

Well-inflated car tyres protect the shock absorbers

This concept can be easily understood by comparing it to car tyres. When tyres are properly inflated, the car runs smoothly without any wobble. However, if the tyres are underinflated, the car is more likely to wobble while in motion. This wobbling places extra strain on both the tyres and the shock absorbers, causing them to wear out more quickly.

EXERCISE REJUVENATES AND MAKES US HEALTHIER

Strong muscles protect our joints

Similarly strong muscles play a crucial role in protecting our joints. During everyday movements, the muscles surrounding a joint help guide it along a smooth, controlled path. When these muscles are weak, joint movements can become unstable, and over time, this repeated instability may lead to joint damage. Pain from early osteoarthritis often discourages movement, which then leads to further muscle weakness, creating a vicious cycle that accelerates joint deterioration. This is why it is so important to keep exercising and strengthening the muscles, even when arthritis is present. Crucially, there is no scientific evidence to suggest that exercise worsens arthritis. That is a common myth — and one that must be firmly laid to rest.

Occasional flares

Occasionally, we may experience increased pain in our joints. However most bone and joint pain will resolve if we slowly exercise and build our muscles. Movement and exercise are essential for the cells in our body to rejuvenate and repair. Increased movement improves blood flow. Improved blood flow provides better nutrition to the joint to nourish and repair itself. Even if the pain is excessive, research shows that the pain will decrease naturally. The level of pain in osteoarthritis may go up and down. Patients report that some days, their symptoms are worse, and some days, their symptoms are less. Occasionally, there may even be a complete lack of symptoms. This is all normal.

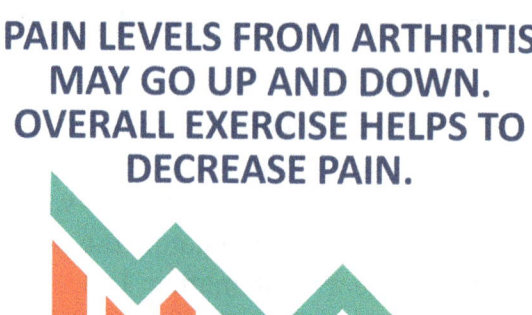

We have now completed the first part of this guide, and I hope you feel more aware of the causes of your pain. We will now move onto how we can start to manage our pain and treat our symptoms effectively.

Part 2

The evidence-based arguments for exercising your pain away

Our joints have life and can repair themselves

If we graze the skin on the outside of our knees, our bodies can repair the damage. This is also true of our joints. This means there is scope for joint regeneration, and our bodies can reverse some of the damage sustained. We also know that exercising and staying active can help to delay the onset and progression of diseases such as arthritis.

Objects without life cannot repair themselves

Objects, like our cars, do not have life and do not have the ability to repair themselves. If a car is scratched just above the wheel on the fender it will not be able to fix itself. It will require some repairs; however, minor the scratch may be. This is why "wear and repair" is a more appropriate term to use for our joints, as the joints can heal or repair naturally. Exercise helps to allow the joint to repair and fix itself.

Can I exercise if I already have arthritis?

Yes, you can—and you should! Many patients believe that once they develop arthritis, they should stop moving to avoid making things worse. However, this is not true. In fact, movement is essential. Research indicates that even in cases of severe arthritis, exercise can reduce pain and improve function. Staying active also helps prevent muscle weakness that can result from prolonged inactivity. Unfortunately, excessive rest can accelerate the decline in both joint health and overall well-being. Maintaining good cardiovascular fitness and general health is particularly important if surgery becomes necessary.

"I HAVE ARTHRITIS, I SHOULDN'T MOVE"

"I AM WAITING FOR A HIP REPLACEMENT, I NEED TO KEEP FIT"

Can I exercise if I am on the list for a hip replacement?

Yes you can! Preoperative exercise, often referred to as "prehabilitation," is now adopted in many centres as part of the preparation for hip replacement surgery. Strengthening the muscles around the hip joint through targeted exercises can enhance joint support and stability, potentially slowing the progression of arthritis-related damage. Regular physical activity may also help to reduce pain and lessen the reliance on painkillers. This is especially important, as long-term use of certain pain medications can negatively affect the kidneys and heart. In some cases, prehabilitation may even delay the need for surgery or help avoid it altogether.

Runners study

An interesting study was conducted in America called the Runners Study[1]. It enrolled two groups of people over the age of 50. One group consisted of 538 runners, and the control group consisted of 423 healthy subjects who were non-runners. The study followed both groups for 21 years.

The study found more cases of osteoarthritis and joint pain in the non-running group than in the running group. In addition, after 19 years of the 21-year study, the number of non-runners who had died was twice the number of runners who had died.

RUNNING DECREASES THE CHANCE OF DEVELOPING OSTEOARTHRITIS

POOR LIFESTYLE CHOICES INCREASES JOINT PAIN

Running decreases arthritis and increases longevity

This study demonstrated that running regularly decreased the rate of arthritis and increased longevity. In fact, normal running protects the joints and provides healthy longevity. Though gentle jogging or running can help, it may not be easy for everyone. The following pages will explain which exercise is best for osteoarthritis. However, a poor lifestyle of inactivity and sedentariness will increase the chance of developing osteoarthritis.

Exercise as a painkiller - 1

Exercise decreases pain in two different ways. The first is by suppressing the pain signal reaching the brain. The pain signal usually moves through a sequence of nerve cells or neurons to finally reach the brain. The signal moves from one cell to the other using chemicals called neurotransmitters. Exercise can dampen down the propagation of the pain signal by modifying the neurotransmitters at the nerve junctions.

EXERCISE CAN MODIFY AND DECREASE THE PAIN SIGNAL BEFORE IT REACHES THE BRAIN

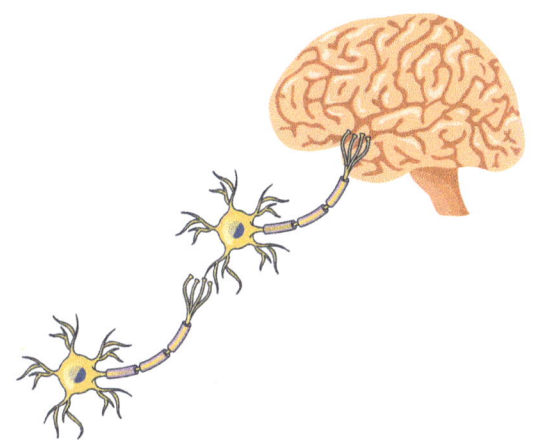

ENDOCANNABINOIDS, THE BODY'S OWN NATURAL PAIN KILLER IS RELEASED IN THE BRAIN DURING EXERCISE

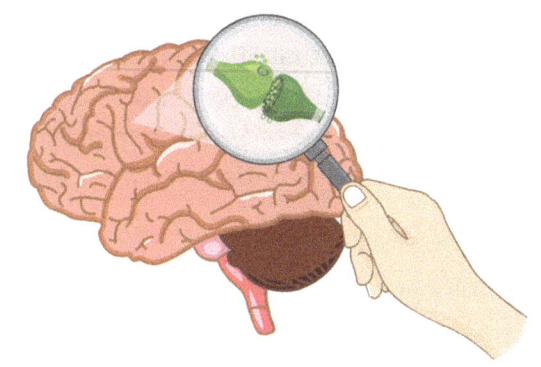

Exercise as a painkiller - 2

The second method involves releasing a natural painkiller called endocannabinoids. This is only released when we exercise[2]. It not only decreases pain but also elevates one's mood. Endocannabinoids released by the brain are why runners feel so jubilant at the end of a run. This is termed the runner's high.

Painkillers can be reduced or even stopped

Exercise may also help reduce the need for painkillers. A study[3] from 2014 showed that 52% of the patients with hip and knee arthritis participating in an exercise and education programme decreased their use of painkillers, of which 18% were able to stop the painkillers altogether. Nearly one-third of the patients using opioids and morphine were able to give it up. Just like with medication, it is important to stick to a routine to get a therapeutic benefit. The best part about using exercise as a therapy is that you will not get the side effects of medicines.

PAINKILLER USE CAN BE REDUCED WITH EXERCISE

40% OF PATIENTS MAY NOT NEED SURGERY WITH EXERCISE

Surgery may not be required

More importantly, surgery may not be required if the exercise builds up the muscles around our joints. Research suggests that some patients can control their symptoms and may not need surgery. A 2021 study[4] found that 40% of patients listed for a total hip replacement surgery and who underwent an exercise and education programme did not require surgery or deferred it for 2 years.

What if exercise does not completely restore your function?

If exercise fails to benefit you, a hip replacement is one of the operations typically performed for advanced hip arthritis. In this operation, both the ball and socket of the hip joint are replaced. Around 100,000 hip replacements are performed in the UK annually.

Although this is a good operation from a scientific perspective, there is patient dissatisfaction following hip replacements. Research[5] estimates that 7-20% of patients who have undergone total hip replacement are dissatisfied with their outcomes.

TOTAL HIP REPLACEMENT

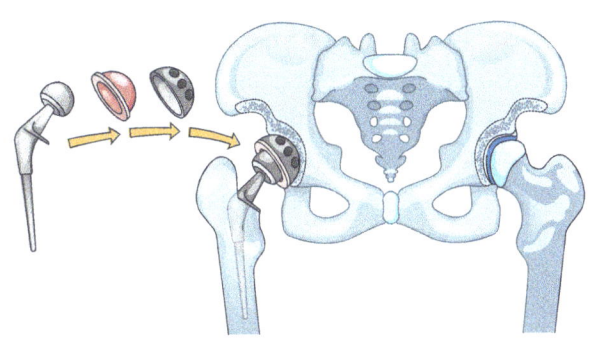

STRONGER MUSCLES INCREASES BLOOD SUPPLY AND ENHANCES REGENERATION

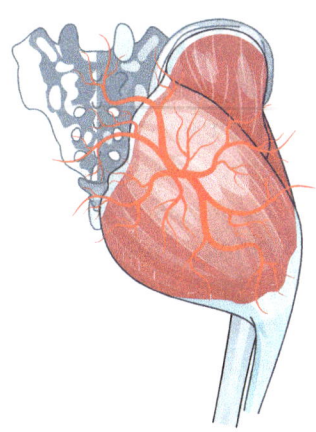

Exercise before surgery can improve the results of surgery

Engaging in prehabilitation—targeted exercises and education before total hip replacement—offers many benefits. It enhances postoperative recovery by helping patients walk and recover sooner. Strong muscles allow the wounds to heal faster. Additionally, it reduces preoperative anxiety and boosts confidence, providing patients with a greater sense of control over their surgical journey. By preparing both body and mind, prehabilitation supports a smoother, safer recovery and promotes better overall outcomes following surgery.

Exercise before surgery can decrease complications

Engaging in prehabilitation reduces the risk of wound leakage and infection. It improves pain control, often lowering the need for medications. Prehab also decreases the chance of developing blood clots in the legs, which can travel to the lungs. It helps shorten hospital stays and reduces the risk of hospital-acquired infections. By improving strength, mobility, and overall fitness, prehabilitation lowers the likelihood of complications and the need for further surgery.

WOUNDS HEAL UP QUICKLY IF PATIENTS HAVE EXERCISED BEFORE SURGERY

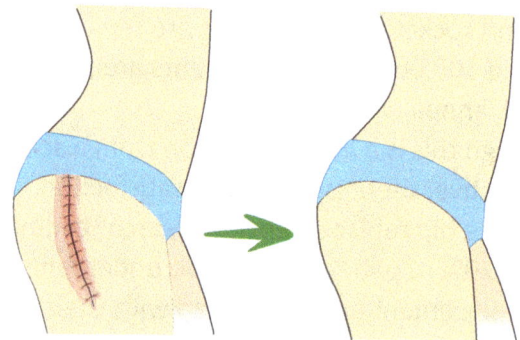

SURGERY THROUGH STRONGER MUSCLES GIVES BETTER RESULTS

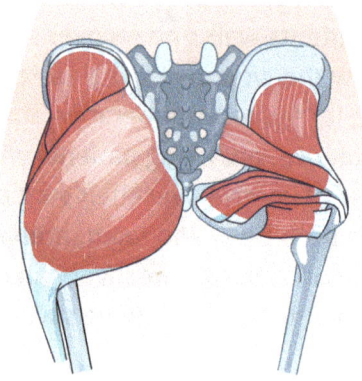

What do surgeons prefer?

"Prehab," or prehabilitation, refers to rehabilitation before surgery. Most surgeons encourage their patients to engage in prehab because it helps prepare the body and mind for the procedure. Surgery through stronger muscles provides superior outcomes. Prehab typically involves three key components: increased physical activity, appropriate dietary changes, and enhanced psychological well-being[6]. Prehabilitation has shown great success in cancer treatment, with research demonstrating improved outcomes for patients who undergo prehab. While it also offers clear benefits in orthopaedic surgery, it is, unfortunately, not yet widely adopted in this field.

Vicious cycle

Sometimes, when we are in pain, we do not move our joints. When we do not move our joints, the muscles become weak. When the muscles become weak, they do not support the joints. When there is less support for the joints, there is more pain. This is a vicious cycle.

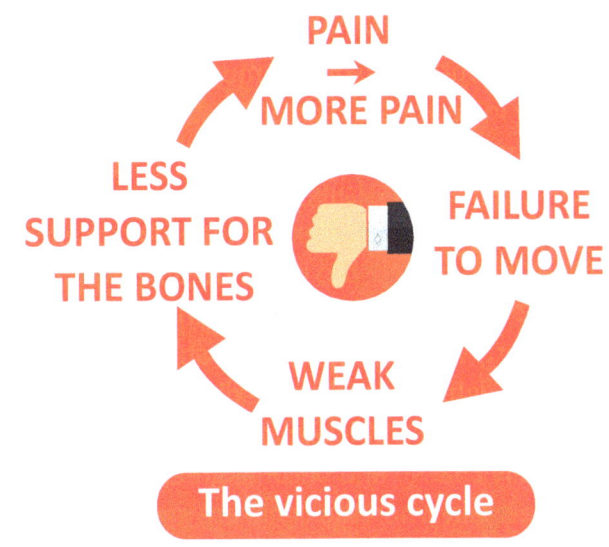

The vicious cycle

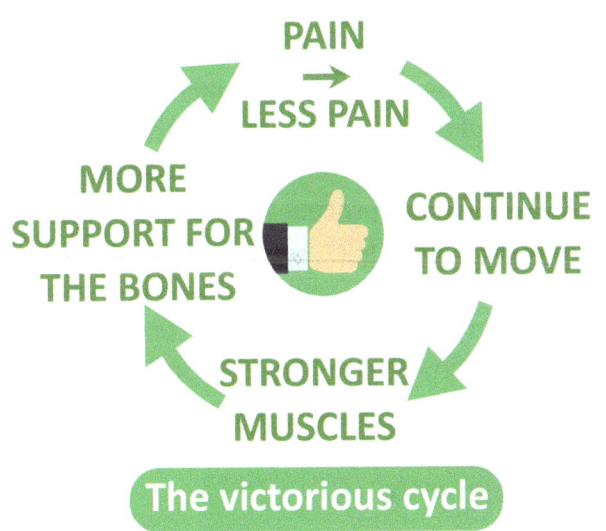

The victorious cycle

Victorious cycle

It is important to convert the vicious cycle into a victorious cycle. Even if we experience pain, we need to exercise. Exercising even a little bit is important. A little exercise builds the muscles ever so slightly. The increased strength in the muscles supports the joints better. The better support decreases the pain. This is how we can convert the vicious cycle to a victorious cycle.

When should I stop exercising?

It is important not to do too much. Doing too much will only increase the pain. Increased pain may prevent you from continuing with the exercise. That will not be helpful. Using the traffic signal is a good method to follow while exercising. You can exercise if there is no pain or the lights are on green. When the light turns orange or you experience increasing discomfort, you must prepare to stop. Don't move when the lights are red or the discomfort changes to pain. Like in a traffic signal, the red light will eventually change and become green. You can exercise again when the lights are green or the pain has subsided.

TRAFFIC LIGHT SYSTEM FOR EXERCISING

EXERCISE LITTLE BUT OFTEN

Slow and steady progress

Slowly and gradually, you need to increase the repetitions and the intensity of the exercise. It is not a quick process and may take time. As explained earlier, the process that occurs in our joints is "wear and repair". For this repair process to occur, movement is essential. Rest in between periods of exercise is also important. Increased movement improves blood flow. Improved blood flow provides better nutrition for the joint. The rest between exercise periods will allow the joint to repair and rejuvenate.

Part 3

The ARISE plan - an exercise programme designed for you

What exercises should I perform to help with arthritis of the hip?

Patients sometimes believe that exercises like walking and swimming will help with hip arthritis. While walking and swimming can help with the symptoms of hip arthritis, neuromuscular exercises may provide better benefits. This is because neuromuscular exercises also improve sensory feedback whilst increasing muscle strength. Studies have identified that in addition to the weakness of muscles in osteoarthritis, there is also derangement of the sensory input from the joint. Neuromuscular exercises are better because they improve both the muscle strength and the sensory input from the joint.

NEUROMUSCULAR EXERCISES FOR HIP ARTHRITIS

OUR BRAIN NEEDS SENSORY INPUT FROM THE JOINT TO MAINTAIN BALANCE AND POSTURE

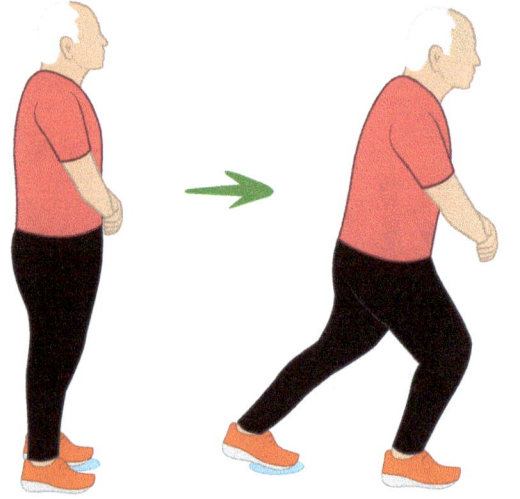

Neuromuscular exercises

In the image on the left, the hip and knee move through different positions as the foot slides over the floor. During these movements, the nerves from the joint send the position of the joint to the brain. This includes the position of the joint, the forces acting across the joint and the rate of any joint movement. Our brain needs this information to adapt and recruit different muscle groups during the movement and to maintain stability and balance. This sensation is called proprioception. This sensory input is deranged in osteoarthritis.

Sensory input from various parts

Whilst performing this exercise, as the hip and the knee joints send the information about the joint to the brain, the nerves in the feet also send the sensory input from the foot's reaction to the floor. The brain collates and merges all this information, and that is how it improves the sense of joint position. This in turn will increase stability and balance.

THE BRAIN MERGES THE INFORMATION FROM THE KNEE AND THE FEET TO IMPROVE BALANCE

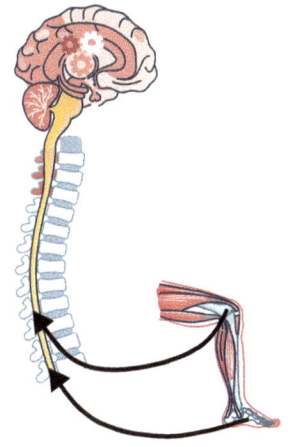

Slides provide the best neuromuscular feedback

Many exercises do have a neuromuscular component. Even swimming and walking have a neuromuscular component. However, slides provide better proprioceptive feedback to train the brain and the body. In slides, the feet are sliding on the floor, and the muscles lift and lower the body. This dual action provides the feedback while lifting and lowering the body weight.

The ARISE Plan

I have created a simple exercise programme called ARISE, based on neuromuscular exercises, to alleviate the pain in your hip caused by arthritis. There are four different groups of exercises, involving 12 different movements in total. We will cover them all in detail.

A - Awareness of the body
R - Resistance and strengthening exercises
I - The "I" in the centre is you!
S - Stability of the core
E - Essential and functional exercises

ARISE NEUROMUSCULAR EXERCISE PROGRAMME

- AWARENESS
- RESISTANCE
- "I" - THAT IS YOU
- STABILITY
- ESSENTIAL

YOU ARE IN THE CENTRE AND WE WANT YOU TO WIN

The "I" in the centre

The letter "I" is at the centre of our ARISE plan. My hope is that by making you the centre of our plan, you can find the strength to arise from the constraints of disability, function better in day-to-day life, and be free from pain. I have faith in you and believe you can do it. Our ARISE plan is designed to be tailored to your needs so that you can reach your goals. For most exercises, we have two levels, and in addition, we have five stages which you can work through. You can begin at the level and stage you are comfortable with and progress when you feel confident to move forward.

Levels of exercise

Each exercise or movement may have one or two levels. Level 1 is an easier version of the exercise, and level 2 is a more difficult version of the same exercise. It is important to concentrate on Level 1 exercises when you start the ARISE plan. After you can comfortably and repeatedly perform Level 1 exercises, you can progress to Level 2.

On the right, you can see me doing both "levels" of the same exercise. In the first image, I am holding the chair for support. Holding the chair in front makes it easier to perform the exercise. Once you are comfortable and confident, the same exercise can be done without the support, as shown in the second image.

Stages of the exercise programme

In addition to the levels of each exercise, there are stages for the entire exercise programme. The stages relate to the repetitions and number of times you exercise within the week. This is because the ARISE plan is designed to enable every single individual to achieve their goals based on how much they can accommodate regular exercise into their lifestyle. We have five stages which you can work through. You can begin at the stage you are comfortable with and progress to the next stage when you feel confident to exercise more. We believe that each stage should be continued for a period of three months.

The five stages:
1. Novice
This stage is for complete beginners. No prior experience is needed to start. Performing five repetitions of Exercises 1 to 7 and 10 to 12 counts as one set, while three repetitions of Exercises 8 and 9 also count as one set. At the novice stage, you should perform one or two sets of exercises during each session. It is helpful to spread your sessions throughout the week, for example, on Mondays, Wednesdays, and Fridays. You can choose the time of day that suits you best for exercising, but it is generally more beneficial to have a consistent time each day.

2. Intermediate
The intermediate stage is designed for those with some exercise experience or for individuals who feel comfortable after spending three months at the novice stage. Performing five repetitions of Exercises 1 to 7 and 10 to 12 counts as one set, while three repetitions of Exercises 8 and 9 also count as one set. At the intermediate stage, you should complete three to four sets of each exercise during each session, exercising three times a week as before.

3. Advanced
The advanced stage is designed for those with a high level of fitness or for individuals who feel confident after three months at the intermediate stage. Performing five repetitions of Exercises 1 to 7 and 10 to 12 counts as one set, while three repetitions of Exercises 8 and 9 also count as one set. At the advanced stage, you should complete five to six sets of each exercise during every session, exercising three times a week as before.

4. Superior
The superior stage should only be attempted once you feel confident after being at the advanced level for three months. Performing five repetitions of Exercises 1 to 7 and 10 to 12 counts as one set, while three repetitions of Exercises 8 and 9 also count as one set. At the superior stage, you perform five to six sets of each exercise during each session, and you exercise four times a week. You may wish to exercise on Mondays, Wednesdays, Fridays, and Sundays.

5. Distinguished
The distinguished stage should only be attempted once you feel confident after being at the superior stage for three months. Performing five repetitions of Exercises 1 to 7 and 10 to 12 counts as one set, while three repetitions of Exercises 8 and 9 also count as one set. At the superior stage, you perform five to six sets of each exercise during each session, and you exercise five times a week. You may wish to exercise on Mondays, Wednesdays, Thursdays, Fridays, and Sundays.

Please note that you do not need to go up a level and a stage at the same time. You can choose to remain at the same level and move up a stage or vice versa.

Let us go through a few examples to illustrate how the levels and stages work.

Example 1

An 80-year-old frail female will start at Level 1 and Stage 1 (Novice). After three months, she stays at Level 1 but progresses to Stage 2 (Intermediate). She is unable to increase the levels or stages further. She now continues with the exercises permanently at Level 1 and Stage 2. If one cannot, there is no need to increase the levels or the stage.

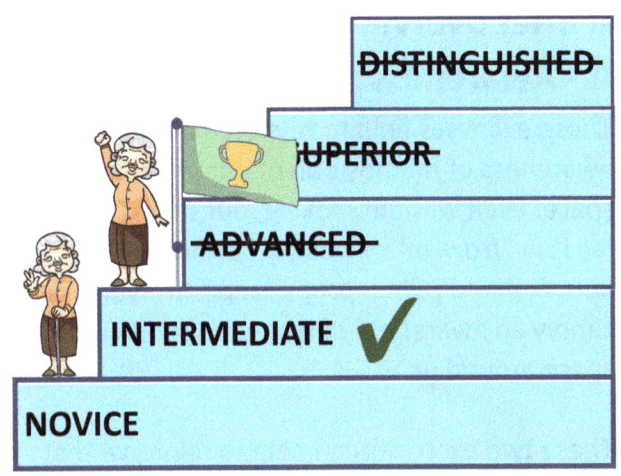

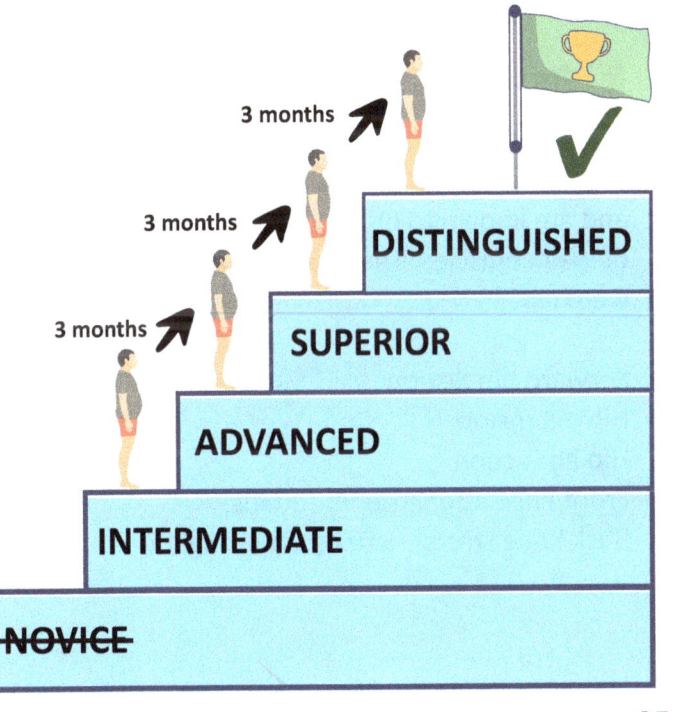

Example 2

A 50-year-old male starts the exercises at Level 1 Stage 2 (Intermediate). Every three months he progresses a stage, and finally reaches Level 2, Stage 5 (Distinguished). He now continues to maintain the exercises permanently at that level and stage.

This programme is designed to be led by you. If you feel that you started at the wrong level or stage, then you can change it. If you feel you have reached your peak, feel free to remain at that level. If you feel you have to drop down a level, you can do that too. It is, however, important to continue exercising regularly at the level and stage you have reached. The point is that you need to feel confident in knowing what your body can do.

A brief overview of the 12 exercises
A - Awareness of the body exercises

These exercises help to reinforce our brain's awareness of the position of our joints and limbs in space. Even without looking, our brains know if our leg is in "front of" or behind our body. That knowledge is called 'proprioception', which is simply an awareness of where our body is in the space around us.

These two exercises can help to reinforce that knowledge:

Backward slides
Side slides

Sliders

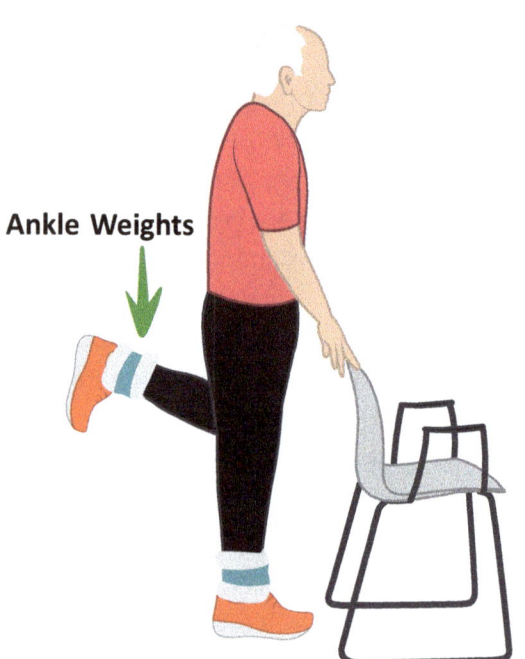
Ankle Weights

R - Resistance and strengthening exercises

These exercises are performed against resistance and are known to quickly increase the strength of weak muscles. These are done with ankle weights.

Forward hip flexion
Hip extension
Hip abduction
Front knee strengthener (quads)
Back knee strengthener (hamstrings)

S - Stability of the core exercises

The core of the body includes the pelvis and lower back. It also includes the abdominal muscles, the muscles surrounding the spine, the diaphragm, and the thigh muscles. A strong core allows the limbs to move more easily.

These exercises will improve core strength:

Side plank
Back plank

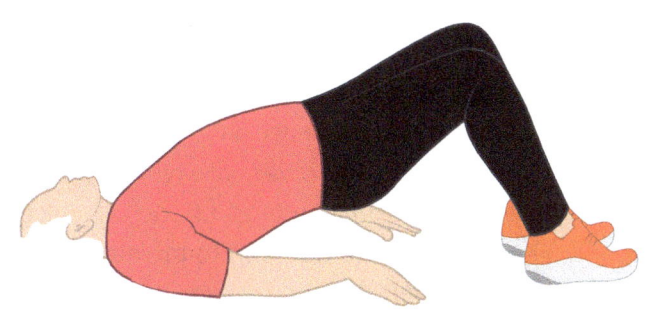

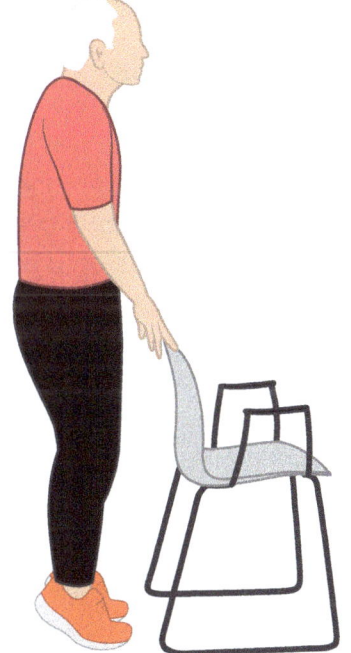

E - Essential and functional exercises.

Our typical daily activities involve getting into and out of a chair often.
When someone has arthritis, getting up from a chair can be more difficult due to pain, and they may need a higher chair to make it easier.
These exercises can help us regain the ability to stand up from a sitting position, regardless of the chair's height.

Knee bends
Heel raises (tiptoeing)
Sit to stand

Equipment that you will need for these exercises

Ankle weights

These small sacks containing sand can be strapped around the ankles with Velcro. To start with, we recommend that you purchase a 0.5 kg or a 1kg pair. As your strength improves, you can progress through different weight options, i.e., 1.5 kg, 2 kg, and 2.5 kg. However, do not rush to increase the weights. Remember, slow and steady wins the race. "Too soon" and "too fast" would be "a boom and bust".

ANKLE WEIGHTS

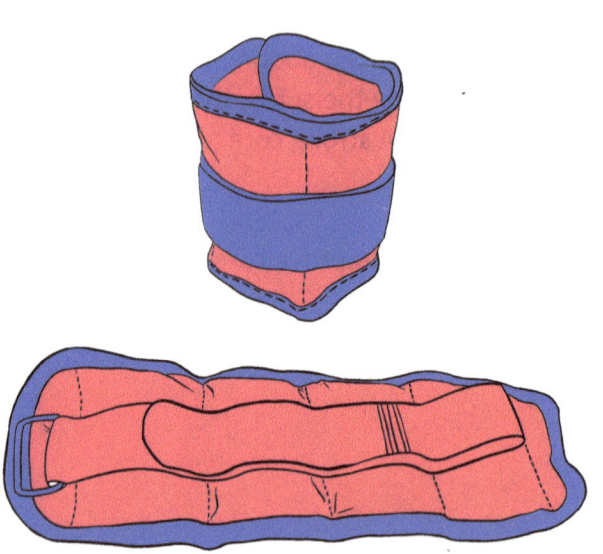

SLIDING DISCS

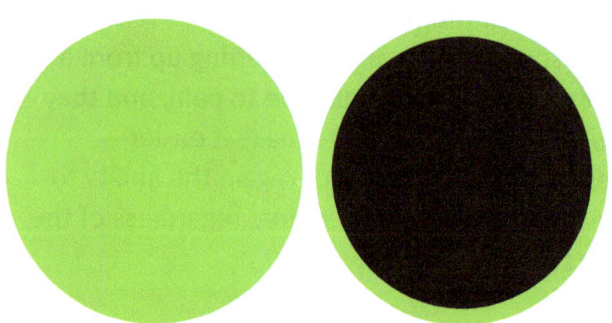

The green plastic side can slide on soft surfaces (e.g. carpet), and the black foam side can slide on hard surfaces (e.g. laminate flooring).

Sliding discs

These are round, flat discs made of plastic about the size of a hand. They are used in sliding exercises, where you can place one foot on top of them and slide them over the ground. One side is shiny, helping the disc slide easily over carpets. The other side is fluffy and can be used over hard floors.

Stable chair with armrests

A stable chair with arms and a high enough backrest to hold from behind.

A table / Zimmer frame

You can hold onto a table or a Zimmer frame (please apply the brakes if they have wheels) if that is more comfortable than holding the back of a chair.

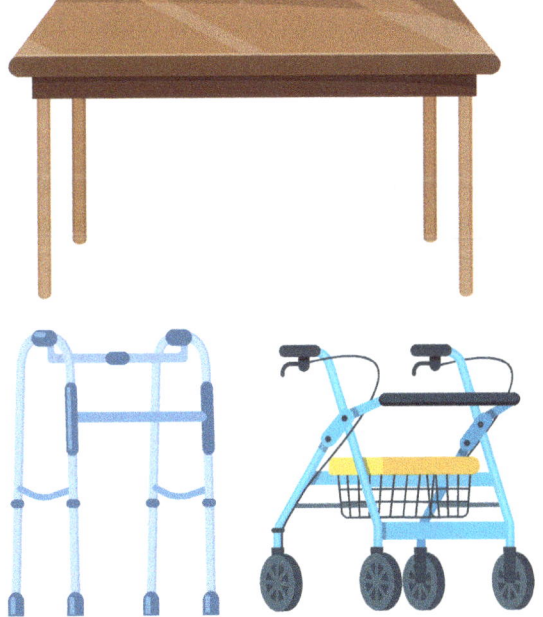

Guide Before You Start Exercising

First and foremost:
- You should be in good physical condition and be able to participate in the exercises.
- Feel free to let your doctor know that you plan to start this functional rehabilitation programme.
- Keep a phone (ideally in your pocket) or any other method of contact close to hand, especially if you are doing it alone. This is just so that you have options if you need help at any time.

Where should I do the exercise?
- We recommend choosing a room with no obstructions on the floor. There should also be no rugs that you could trip over! If you have a pet in the house, you might feel more comfortable if they are in another room so that you do not trip over them.

What should I wear?
- Dress comfortably. Nothing tight or restricting. Your trouser legs should not touch the floor so you do not trip on the bottom. We recommend wearing trainers or shoes that fit well.

What do I need to exercise?
- The exercises are designed to be done in a standard living room at home with minimal equipment. The only equipment you need are some chairs or a table or a Zimmer frame, ankle weights (0.5 or 1 kg on each leg to start with) and sliding discs. The ankle weights and the sliding discs should be available in sports stores or on Amazon.

It is normal to feel quite tired after the exercises. You have been moving your body and getting your heart pumping after all! Take it easy. Make sure to rest. It is vital to give your body time to recover before the next exercise. Always listen to your body - you know yourself best, so trust your instincts!

Part 4

The 12 Exercises

Exercise 1 - Backward slide
Level 1 (supported)

Stand behind a chair facing forward. Hold the back of the chair with both hands and look straight ahead. Place the sliding disc underneath your left foot.

Bend your right knee and hip and lower your body by a few inches while sliding your left foot backwards in a straight line. Stand up and bring your left foot forward to return to your original position. Repeat five times.

Swap legs and repeat five times.

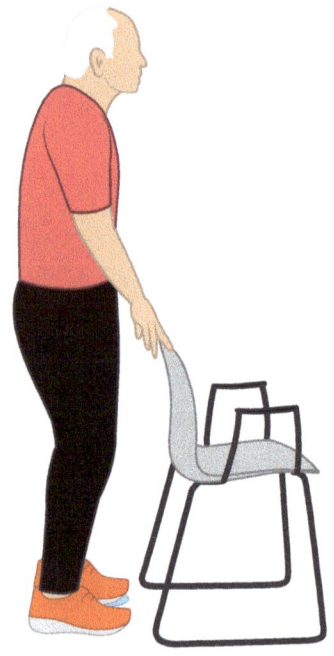

Exercise 1 - Backward slide
Level 2 (without the chair)

Only progress to this level if you are confident with Level 1, described on the previous page.

You can leave your hands by your side or clasp and hold them about six inches away from your tummy. Place the sliding disc underneath your left foot. Bend your right knee and hip and lower your body by a few inches while sliding your left foot backwards in a straight line. Stand up and bring your left foot forward to return to your original position. Repeat five times.

Swap legs and repeat five times.

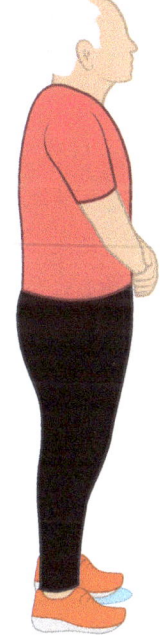

Exercise 2 - Sideward slide
Level 1 (supported)

Stand behind a chair facing forward. Hold the back of the chair with both hands and look straight ahead. Place the sliding disc underneath your left foot.

Bend your right knee and hip and lower your body by a few inches while sliding your left foot towards the left and away from your body in a straight line. Return to your original position by standing up and bringing your left foot towards the centre. Repeat five times.

Swap legs and repeat five times.

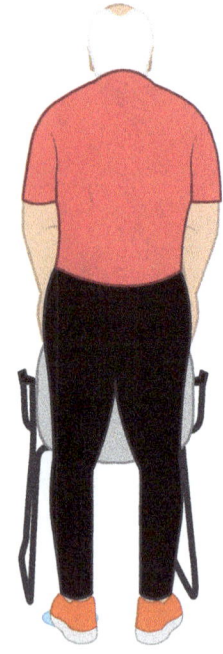
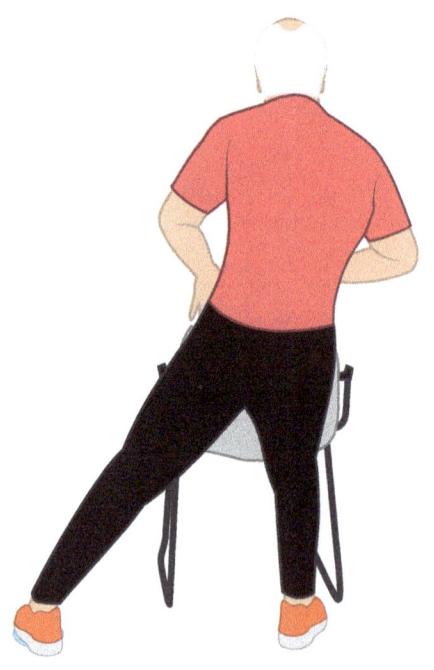

Exercise 2 - Sideward slide
Level 2 (without the chair)

Only progress to this level if you are confident with Level 1, described on the previous page.

You can leave your hands by your side or clasp and hold them about six inches away from your tummy. Bend your right knee and hip and lower your body by a few inches while sliding your left foot towards the left and away from your body in a straight line. Return to your original position by standing up and bringing your left foot towards the centre. Repeat five times.

Swap legs and repeat five times.

Exercise 3 - Hip flexion
Level 1 (supported)

Fasten the ankle weights to both legs. Stand sideways behind a chair with the left side of your body closer to the chair. Hold the back of the chair with your left hand and look straight ahead.

Slowly lift your left leg forward, lifting your foot about 10cm above the ground, then lower it down to the original position. Lower your leg slightly slower than raising your leg. Count to two to lift and three to return to the original position. Repeat five times.

Swap legs and repeat five times.

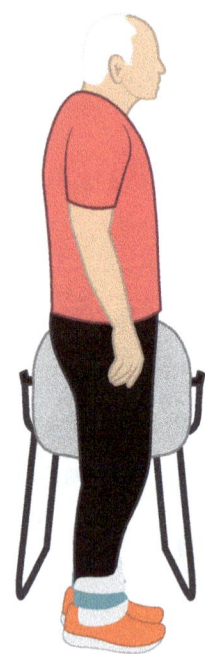

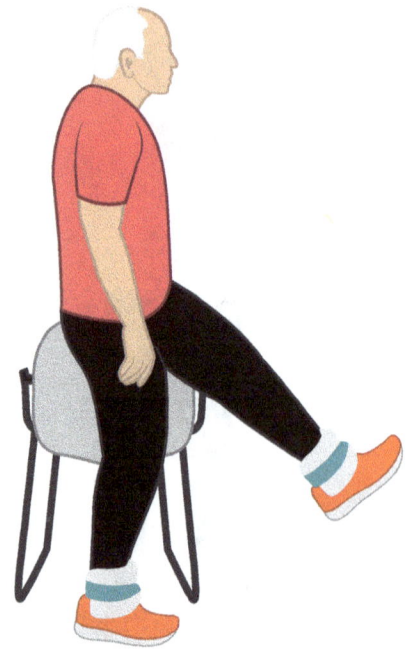

Exercise 3 - Hip flexion
Level 2 (without the chair)

Only progress to this level if you are confident with Level 1, described on the previous page.

Fasten the ankle weights to both legs. Stand upright and look straight ahead. You can leave your hands by your side or clasp them together in front of you.

Slowly lift your left leg forward, lifting your foot about 10cm above the ground, then lower it down to the original position. Lower your leg slightly slower than raising your leg. Count to two to lift and three to return to the original position. Repeat five times.

Swap legs and repeat five times.

Exercise 4 - Hip extension
Level 1 (supported)

Fasten the ankle weights to both legs. Stand sideways behind a chair with the left side of your body closer to the chair. Hold the back of the chair with your left hand and look straight ahead.

Slowly lift your left leg backwards in a straight line, lifting your foot about 10cm above the ground. Then, lower it down to the original position. Lower your leg slightly slower than raising your leg. Count to two to lift and three to return to the original position. Repeat five times.

Swap legs and repeat five times.

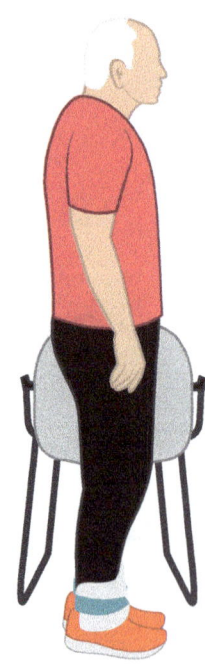
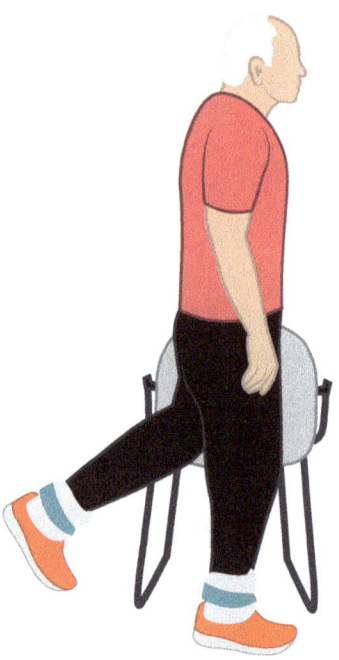

Exercise 4 - Hip extension
Level 2 (without the chair)

Only progress to this level if you are confident with Level 1, described on the previous page.

Fasten the ankle weights to both legs. Stand upright and look straight ahead. You can leave your hands by your side or clasp them together in front of you.

Slowly lift your left leg backwards in a straight line, lifting your foot about 10cm above the ground. Then, lower it down to the original position. Lower your leg slightly slower than raising your leg. Count to two to lift and three to return to the original position. Repeat five times.

Swap legs and repeat five times.

Exercise 5 - Hip abduction
Level 1 (supported)

Fasten the ankle weights to both legs. Stand behind the chair facing forward. Hold the back of the chair with both hands and look straight ahead.

Slowly lift your left leg sideways, lifting your foot about 10cm above the ground. Ensure that your foot is pointing forward, as there is often a tendency for the foot to turn outwards. If it turns outwards, then the wrong muscle is being used. Lower it down to the original position. Lower your leg slightly slower than raising your leg. Count to 2 to lift, and count to 3 to return to the original position. Repeat five times.

Swap legs and repeat 5 times.

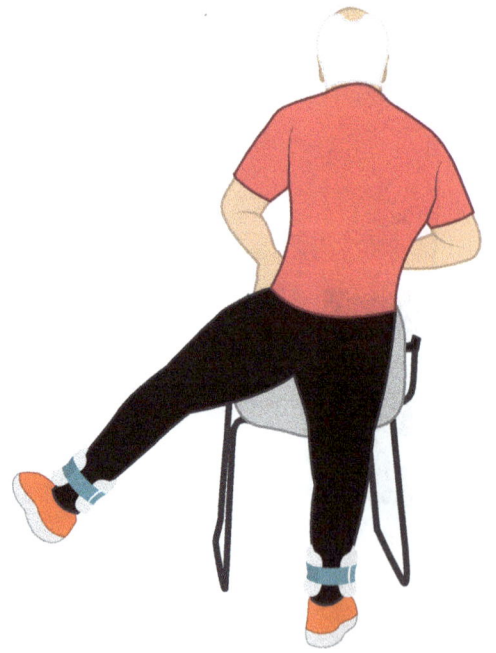

Exercise 5 - Hip abduction
Level 2 (without the chair)

Only progress to this level if you are confident with Level 1, described on the previous page.

Fasten the ankle weights to both legs. Stand upright and look straight ahead. You can leave your hands by your side or clasp them together in front of you.

Slowly lift your left leg sideways, lifting your foot about 10cm above the ground. Ensure that your foot is pointing forward, then lower it down to the original position. Count to two to lift and three to return to the original position. Repeat five times.

Swap legs and repeat five times.

Exercise 6 - Front knee strengthener
Level 1 (supported)

Begin seated with knees bent and feet flat on the floor. Fasten the ankle weights to both legs.

Slowly straighten your left leg. Once it is fully straight, slowly bend it, returning to the starting position. Count to 2 to lift and 3 to return to the original position. Repeat five times.

Swap legs and repeat 5 times.

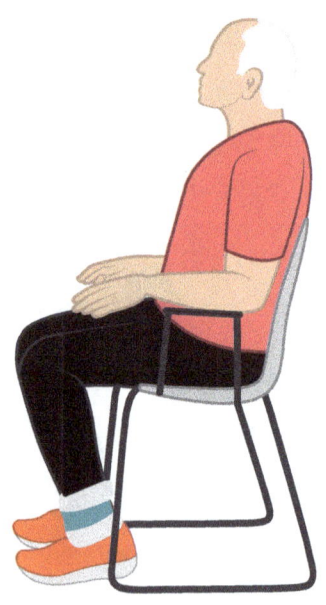
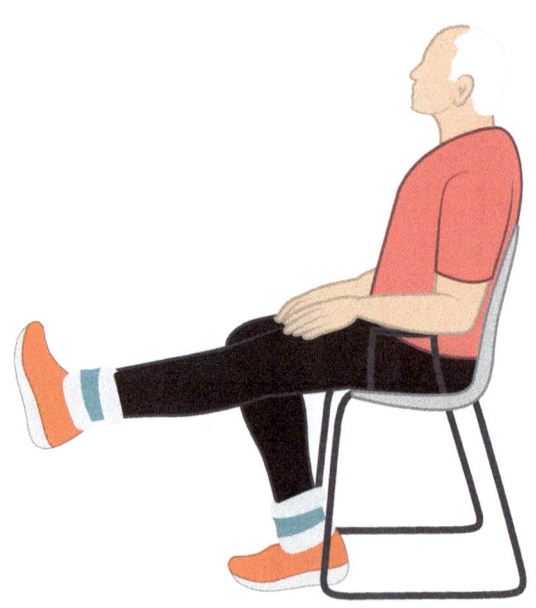

You are doing so well.
Keep on going!

Exercising is a win-win situation.

Exercise 7 - Back knee strengthener Level 1 (supported)

Stand up straight, holding on to the back of a chair. Look straight ahead.

Slowly bend your left knee until it is at a 90-degree angle. Once your left leg is at a right angle to your thigh, slowly lower your foot to the floor.

During the exercise your foot should be lifted backwards by bending your knee. Ensure that your knee/thigh does not move forward during this exercise. Lower your leg slightly slower than raising your leg. Count to 2 to lift and 3 to return to the original position. Repeat five times.

Swap legs and repeat 5 times.

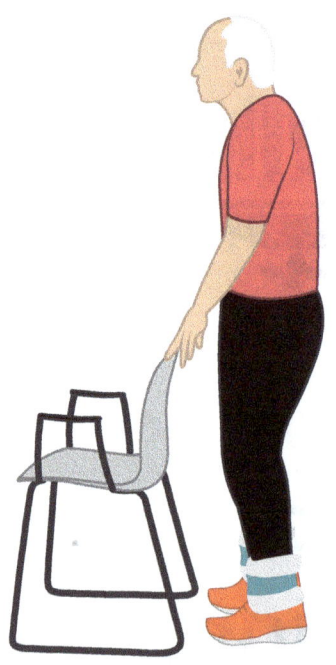
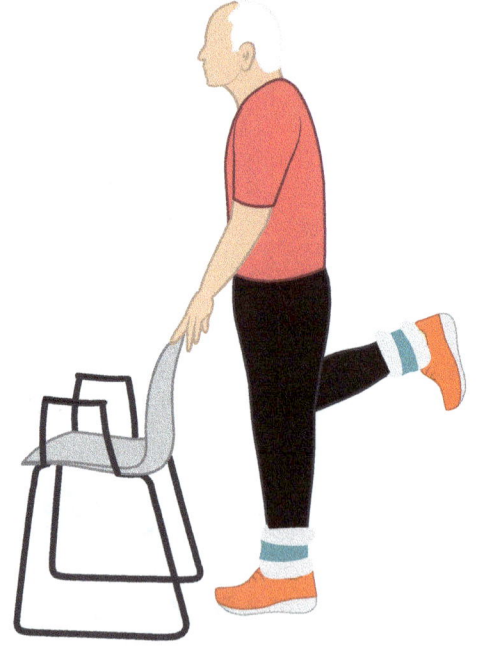

Exercise 7 - Back knee strengthener Level 2 (without the chair)

Only progress to this level if you are confident with Level 1, described on the previous page.

Stand up straight, looking straight ahead. You can leave your hands by your side or clasp them together in front of you.

Slowly bend your left knee until it is at a 90-degree angle. Slowly lower your foot to the floor once your left leg is at a right angle to your thigh.

During the exercise, your foot should be lifted backwards by bending your knee. Ensure that your knee/thigh does not move forward. Lower your leg slightly slower than raising it. Count to two to lift and three to return to the original position. Repeat five times.

Swap legs and repeat five times.

Exercise 8 - Side plank
Level 1 (keeping your knees bent and pivoting on your knee)

This exercise can be done on the floor or the bed. If you are using the bed, use a firm mattress. Lie on your left side and support your upper body using your left elbow. Keep your lower legs bent backwards. Your trunk and thighs should be in line. Draw your belly button towards your spine while pulling up your pelvic floor muscles. Lift your hips, pivoting on your knee until your trunk and thighs reach a straight line. Maintain this position for a count of 10.

Relax and lie back down. Repeat three times. Turnover and repeat three times on the other side.

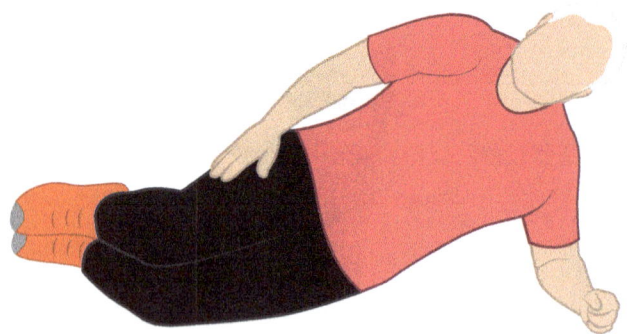
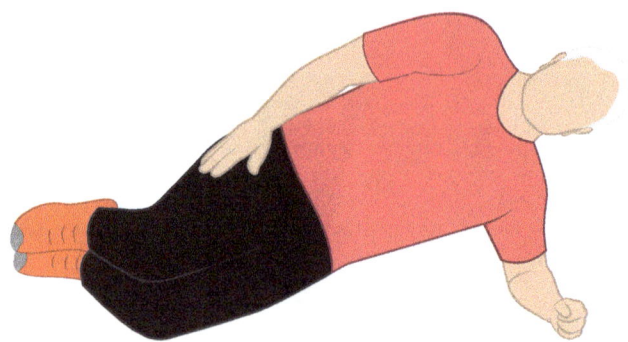

Exercise 8 - Side plank
Level 2 (keeping your knees straight and pivoting on your feet)

Only progress to this level if you are confident with Level 1, described on the previous page.

This exercise can be done on the floor or the bed. If you are using the bed, use a firm mattress. Lie on your left side and support your upper body using your left elbow. Keep your knees straight and place your right foot in front of your left foot. Your trunk, thighs, and lower legs should be in line.

Draw your belly button towards your spine while pulling up your pelvic floor muscles. Lift your hips, pivoting on your feet until your trunk, thighs, and lower legs reach a straight line. Maintain this position for a count of 10.

Relax and lie back down. Repeat three times. Turnover and repeat three times on the other side.

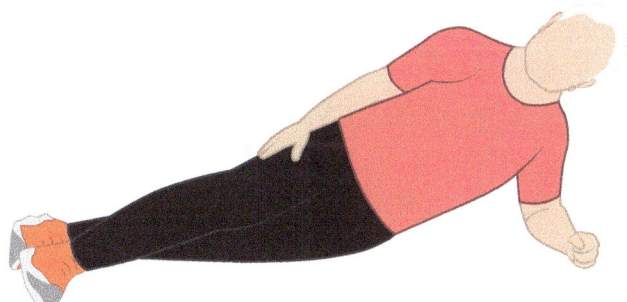
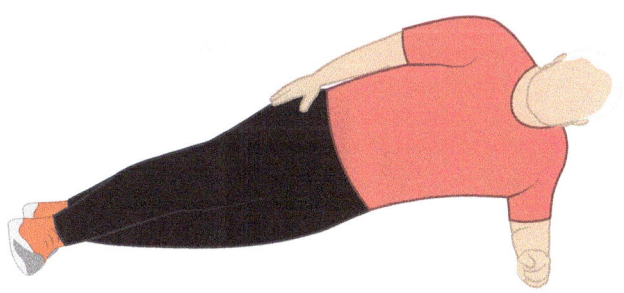

Exercise 9 - Back plank
Level 1 (arms by your side)

Lie on your back with your arms by your side. This exercise can be done on the floor or on the bed. Bend your legs at the knee while keeping your feet flat on the floor.

Draw your belly button towards your spine while pulling up your pelvic floor muscles. Push your hips up off the floor so that your trunk and thighs are in a straight line. Hold this position for a count of 10.

Relax and lie back down. Repeat three times.

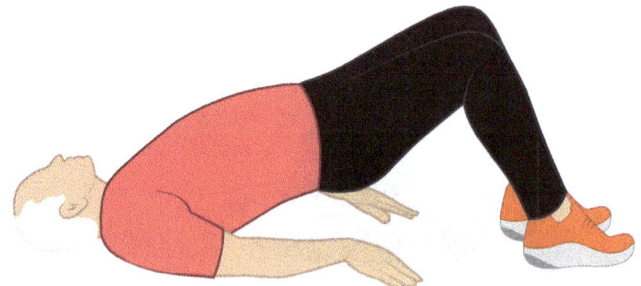

Exercise 9 - Back plank
Level 2 (arms folded in front)

Only progress to this level if you are confident with Level 1, described on the previous page.

Lie on your back with your arms folded in the front of your body. This exercise can be done on the floor or on the bed. Bend your legs at the knee while keeping your feet flat on the floor.

Draw your belly button towards your spine while pulling up your pelvic floor muscles. Push your hips up off the floor so that your trunk and thighs are in a straight line. Hold this position for a count of 10.

Relax and lie back down, then repeat three times.

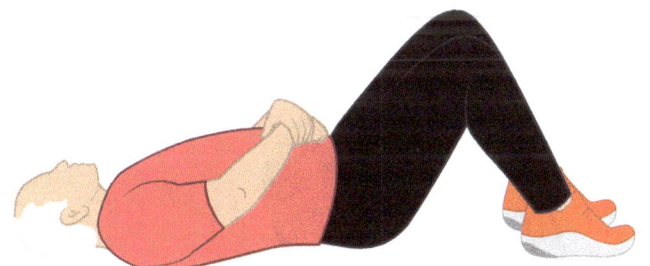
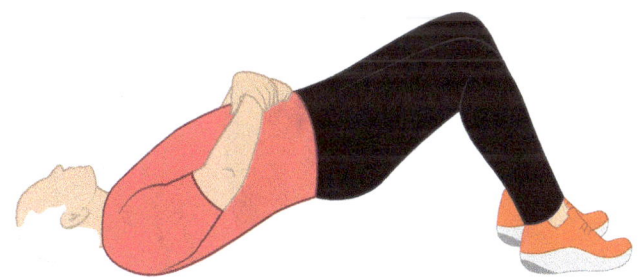

Exercise 10 - Knee bends
Level 1 (supported)

Place two chairs, one behind the other. Stand between them and hold onto the backrest of the chair in front. Stand straight with your feet shoulder-width apart, pointing forwards.

Start by bending both your knees and hips, pushing your buttocks backwards as if attempting to sit down.

Try to keep your knees directly above your feet. Stop when your buttocks reach halfway between the standing and sitting position, ensuring they do not touch the seat. Straighten your knees and hips to return to the starting position.

Repeat this exercise five times.

Initially, it may be difficult to reach halfway between the standing and sitting positions. In this case, only go down an inch or two. As your strength increases, your range of movement will improve with time.

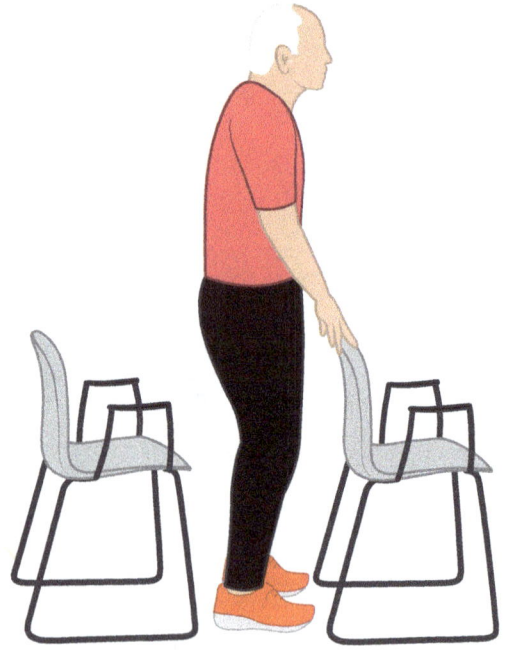

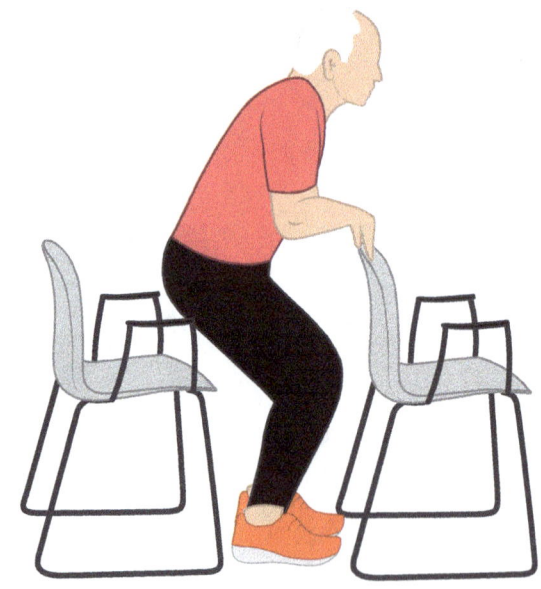

Exercise 10 - Knee bends
Level 2 (without the chair)

Only progress to this level if you are confident with Level 1, described on the previous page.

Stand straight with your feet shoulder-width apart, pointing forwards. You can leave your hands by your side or clasp them together in front of you.

Start by bending both your knees and hips, pushing your buttocks backwards as if attempting to sit down into the chair behind.

Try to keep your knees directly above your feet. Stop when your buttocks reach halfway between the standing and sitting position, ensuring they do not touch the seat. Straighten your knees and hips to return to the starting position.

Repeat five times.

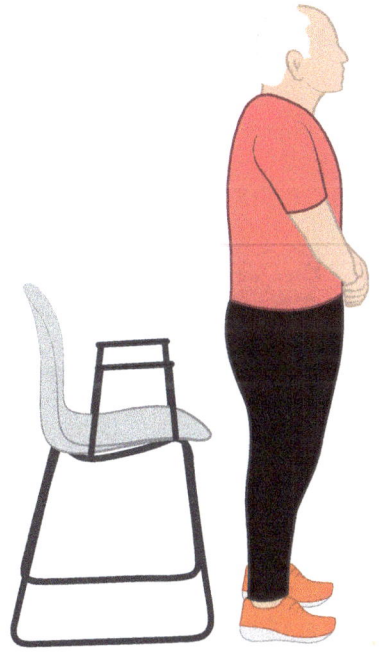

Exercise 11 - Heel raises (tiptoeing)
Level 1 (supported)

Begin by standing behind the back of a chair and holding onto the backrest for support. Then, stand straight with your feet shoulder-width apart.

Slowly raise both heels off the ground on your tiptoes, then slowly lower your heels back down.

Repeat five times.

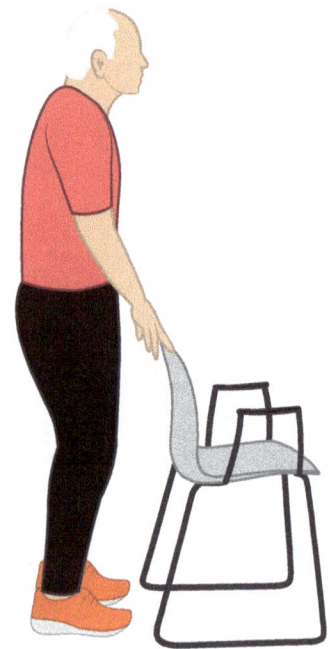
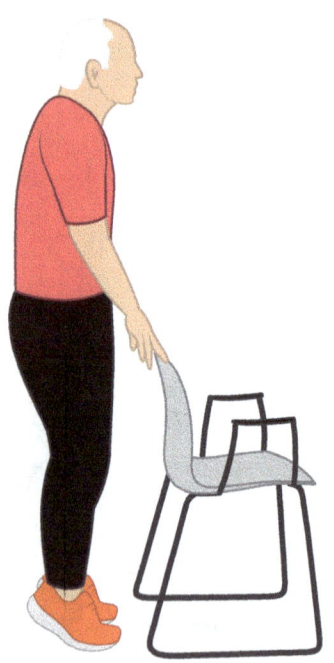

Exercise 11 - Heel raises (tiptoeing)
Level 2 (without the chair)

Only progress to this level if you are confident with Level 1, described on the previous page.

Stand straight with your feet shoulder-width apart. You can leave your hands by your side or clasp them together in front of you.

Slowly raise both heels off the ground onto your tiptoes, then slowly lower your heels back down. Repeat five times.

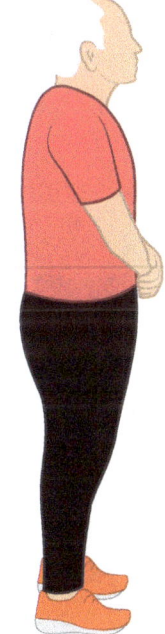

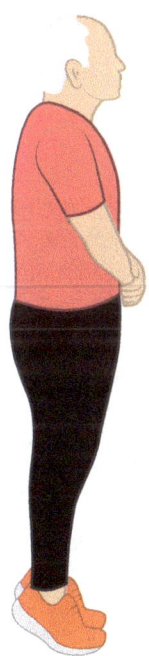

Exercise 12 - Sit to stand
Level 1 (supported)

Sit towards the front of a chair with another chair in front. Bend your knees slightly so that your feet are under your thighs. Tucking your feet in slightly will increase your ability to stand from the sitting position.

Hold onto the back of the chair in front, then stand up from the sitting position. Once upright, slowly sit back down while holding onto the chair in front for support.

Repeat five times.

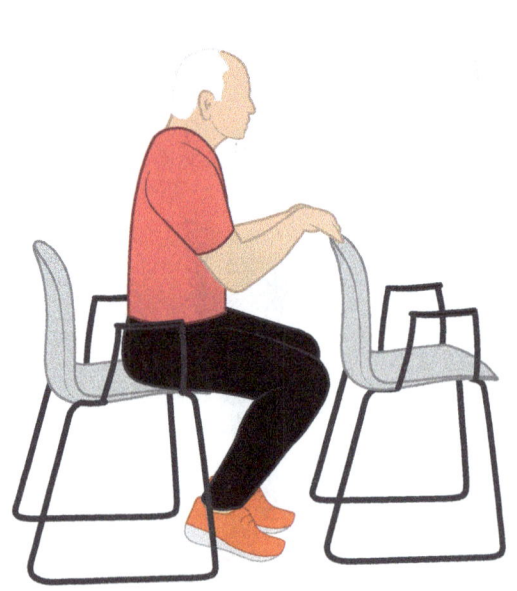

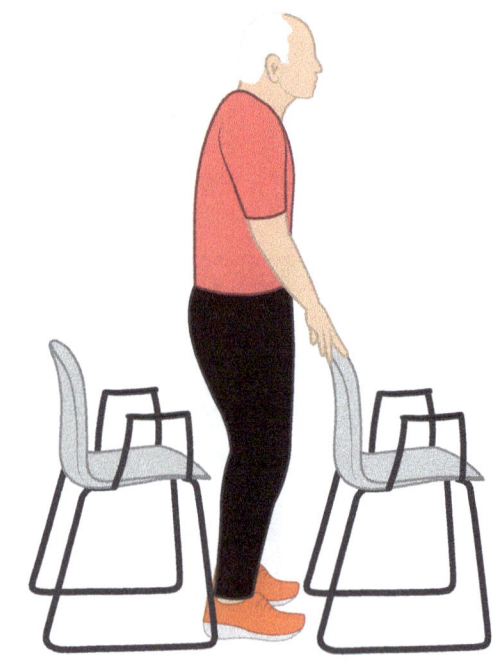

Exercise 12 - Sit to stand
Level 2 (without the extra chair)

Only progress to this level if you are confident with Level 1, described on the previous page.

Sit towards the front of a chair. Bend your knees slightly so that your feet are under your thighs. Rest your hands on your thighs.

Now, stand up from the sitting position. Once you are upright, slowly sit back down.

Repeat five times.

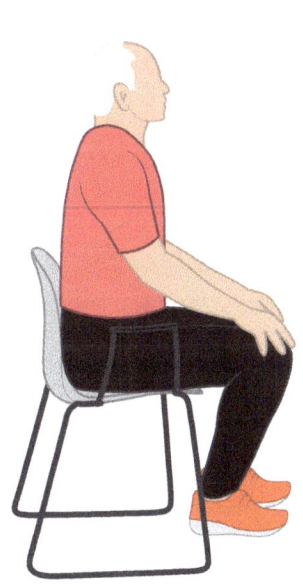

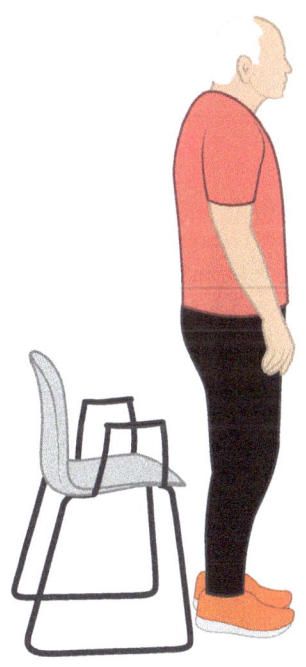

Closing words

I sincerely hope this book has empowered you to regain your ability and confidence. My goal is to enable you to lead a pain-free, stronger, and fulfilling life. The progress you make is credit to you the reader. I want to wish you all the best in this journey.

Best wishes,

George

References

1. Chakravarty EF, Hubert HB, Lingala VB, Fries JF. Reduced Disability and Mortality Among Aging Runners: A 21-Year Longitudinal Study. Arch Intern Med. 2008;168(15):1638-1646. doi:10.1001/archinte.168.15.1638.

2. Matei D, Trofin D, Iordan DA, Onu I, Condurache I, Ionite C, Buculei I. The Endocannabinoid System and Physical Exercise. Int J Mol Sci. 2023 Jan 19;24(3):1989. doi: 10.3390/ijms24031989.

3. Thorlund JB, Roos EM, Goro P, Ljungcrantz EG, Grønne DT, Skou ST. Patients use fewer analgesics following supervised exercise therapy and patient education: an observational study of 16 499 patients with knee or hip osteoarthritis. Br J Sports Med. 2021 Jun;55(12):670-675. doi: 10.1136/bjsports-2019-101265. Epub 2020 Sep 21. PMID: 32958468.

4. Clausen S, Hartvigsen J, Boyle E, et al. Prognostic factors of total hip replacement during a 2-year period in participants enrolled in supervised education and exercise therapy: a prognostic study of 3657 participants with hip osteoarthritis. Arthritis Res Ther. 2021 Sep 7;23(1):235. doi:10.1186/s13075-021-02608-6. PMID: 34493331; PMCID: PMC8422712.

5. Shao Z, Bi S. Patient satisfaction after total hip arthroplasty: Influencing factors. Front Surg. 2023 Jan 30;9:1043508. doi:10.3389/fsurg.2022.1043508. PMID: 36793514; PMCID: PMC9922864.

6. Punnoose A, Claydon-Mueller LS, Weisse O, et al. Prehabilitation for Patients Undergoing Orthopedic Surgery. JAMA Netw Open. 2023;6(4):e238050. doi:10/1001/jamanetworkopen.2023.8050.

7. Ageberg E, Nilsdotter A, Kosek E, Roos EM. Effects of neuromuscular training (NEMEX-TJR) on patient-reported outcomes and physical function in severe primary hip or knee osteoarthritis: a controlled before-and-after study. BMC Musculoskelet Disord. 2013 Aug 8;14:232. doi: 10.1186/1471-2474-14-232. PMID: 23924144; PMCID: PMC3750589.

Name .... Date of starting programme............................

Week 1	Monday	Tuesday	Wed	Thursday	Friday	Saturday	Sunday
Date							
Level / Stage							
Pain on a scale of 10							

Week 2	Monday	Tuesday	Wed	Thursday	Friday	Saturday	Sunday
Date							
Level / Stage							
Pain on a scale of 10							

Week 3	Monday	Tuesday	Wed	Thursday	Friday	Saturday	Sunday
Date							
Level / Stage							
Pain on a scale of 10							

Week 4	Monday	Tuesday	Wed	Thursday	Friday	Saturday	Sunday
Date							
Level / Stage							
Pain on a scale of 10							

Name .... Date of starting programme...........................

Week 5	Monday	Tuesday	Wed	Thursday	Friday	Saturday	Sunday
Date							
Level / Stage							
Pain on a scale of 10							

Week 6	Monday	Tuesday	Wed	Thursday	Friday	Saturday	Sunday
Date							
Level / Stage							
Pain on a scale of 10							

Week 7	Monday	Tuesday	Wed	Thursday	Friday	Saturday	Sunday
Date							
Level / Stage							
Pain on a scale of 10							

Week 8	Monday	Tuesday	Wed	Thursday	Friday	Saturday	Sunday
Date							
Level / Stage							
Pain on a scale of 10							

Name .... Date of starting programme........................

Week 9	Monday	Tuesday	Wed	Thursday	Friday	Saturday	Sunday
Date							
Level / Stage							
Pain on a scale of 10							

Week 10	Monday	Tuesday	Wed	Thursday	Friday	Saturday	Sunday
Date							
Level / Stage							
Pain on a scale of 10							

Week 11	Monday	Tuesday	Wed	Thursday	Friday	Saturday	Sunday
Date							
Level / Stage							
Pain on a scale of 10							

Week 12	Monday	Tuesday	Wed	Thursday	Friday	Saturday	Sunday
Date							
Level / Stage							
Pain on a scale of 10							

Other books by Dr George Ampat

Free Free From Pain Exercise Book - is a practical guide designed to help older adults reduce pain and improve mobility through safe, home-based exercises. It combines medical insights, practical advice, and motivational metaphors to encourage ageing healthily rather than gracefully with greater strength, improved balance, and more independence. The book blends medical insights, clear instructions, and real-life testimonials to encourage a positive, gradual approach to living a more active, pain-free life. ISBN 978-0995676947 Price £18.00

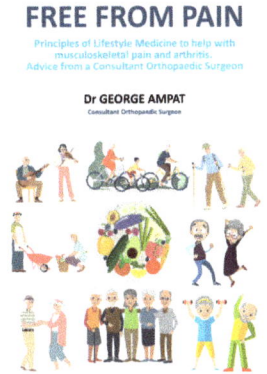

Free From Pain Information Book - Lifestyle medicine offers a sustainable and holistic solution to the musculoskeletal pain epidemic. Rather than relying on a single intervention, lifestyle medicine emphasizes the cumulative power of small, actionable steps. When practiced consistently, these measures can significantly improve symptoms of arthritis and chronic pain. This book identifies 15 key areas of lifestyle medicine that can be effectively utilized to manage arthritis and pain. ISBN 978-0995676954 Price 18.00

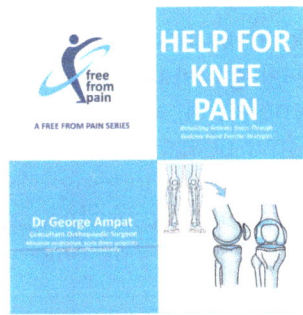

Help for Knee Pain - emphasizes a holistic and sustainable approach to managing knee pain and knee arthritis through structured exercise, education, and proactive self-care. By following the ARISE plan, individuals can reduce pain, strengthen their joints, and improve their quality of life while potentially avoiding surgical interventions. The ARISE plain is a structured program with 12 exercises divided into; Awareness (proprioception training), Resistance (muscle strengthening), I (the individual at the center), Stability (core strength) and Essential functional movements. ISBN 978-0-9956769-8-5 Price £12.00

Help for Hip pain - emphasizes a holistic and sustainable approach to managing hip pain and hip arthritis through structured exercise, education, and proactive self-care. By following the ARISE plan, individuals can reduce pain, strengthen their joints, and improve their quality of life while potentially avoiding surgical interventions. The ARISE plain is a structured program with 12 exercises divided into; Awareness (proprioception training), Resistance (muscle strengthening), I (the individual at the center), Stability (core strength) and Essential functional movements. ISBN 978-0-9956769-7-8 Price £12.00

Other books by Dr George Ampat

Ease the Feet is a comprehensive resource for understanding and managing common foot conditions without surgical intervention. It focuses on using prefabricated orthotics as a practical solution to alleviate pain and improve foot function. The foot conditions discussed in brief are Plantar Fasciitis, Metatarsalgia, Bunions, Diabetes, Sports Injuries and Arthritis. The book also contains 25 exercises designed to strengthen and stretch the feet, improve flexibility, and reduce pain. ISBN 978-0995676961 Price £8.00

Titles being developed

  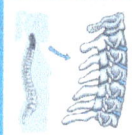

Help for Neck Pain is a practical, evidence-based guide to understanding and relieving neck pain without surgery. With clear explanations and powerful metaphors, this book demystifies spinal anatomy, disc degeneration, and nerve compression. Learn how targeted isometric and resistance exercises can strengthen neck and shoulder muscles, reduce pain, and restore function. Backed by real patient stories and clinical insights, this empowering guide offers safe, effective techniques for long-term relief. Perfect for anyone ready to take control of their neck health naturally and confidently.

  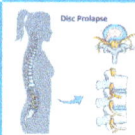

Help for Back Pain is a practical, empowering guide to understanding and overcoming low back pain. With simple explanations, engaging metaphors, and science-backed advice, it covers spinal anatomy, disc degeneration, and sciatica. Learn to retrain key muscles like the multifidus through a four-phase exercise program: Synchrony, Stability, Strength, and Sustain. Whether you're dealing with chronic pain or aiming to prevent it, this book offers effective, accessible tools to regain strength, stability, and a pain-free life—without surgery or long-term medication.

Help for Chronic Pain is a practical and compassionate guide designed to help you manage pain without relying on medication or surgery. Based on the latest research, this book introduces a powerful ten-step program—MY-SELF-HELP—that includes mindfulness, sleep, exercise, nutrition, and emotional well-being. Each chapter offers clear explanations and simple strategies to rewire the brain, reduce pain, and restore joy. Whether you're newly diagnosed or have struggled for years, this book provides the tools to take control and live a fuller, pain-free life.

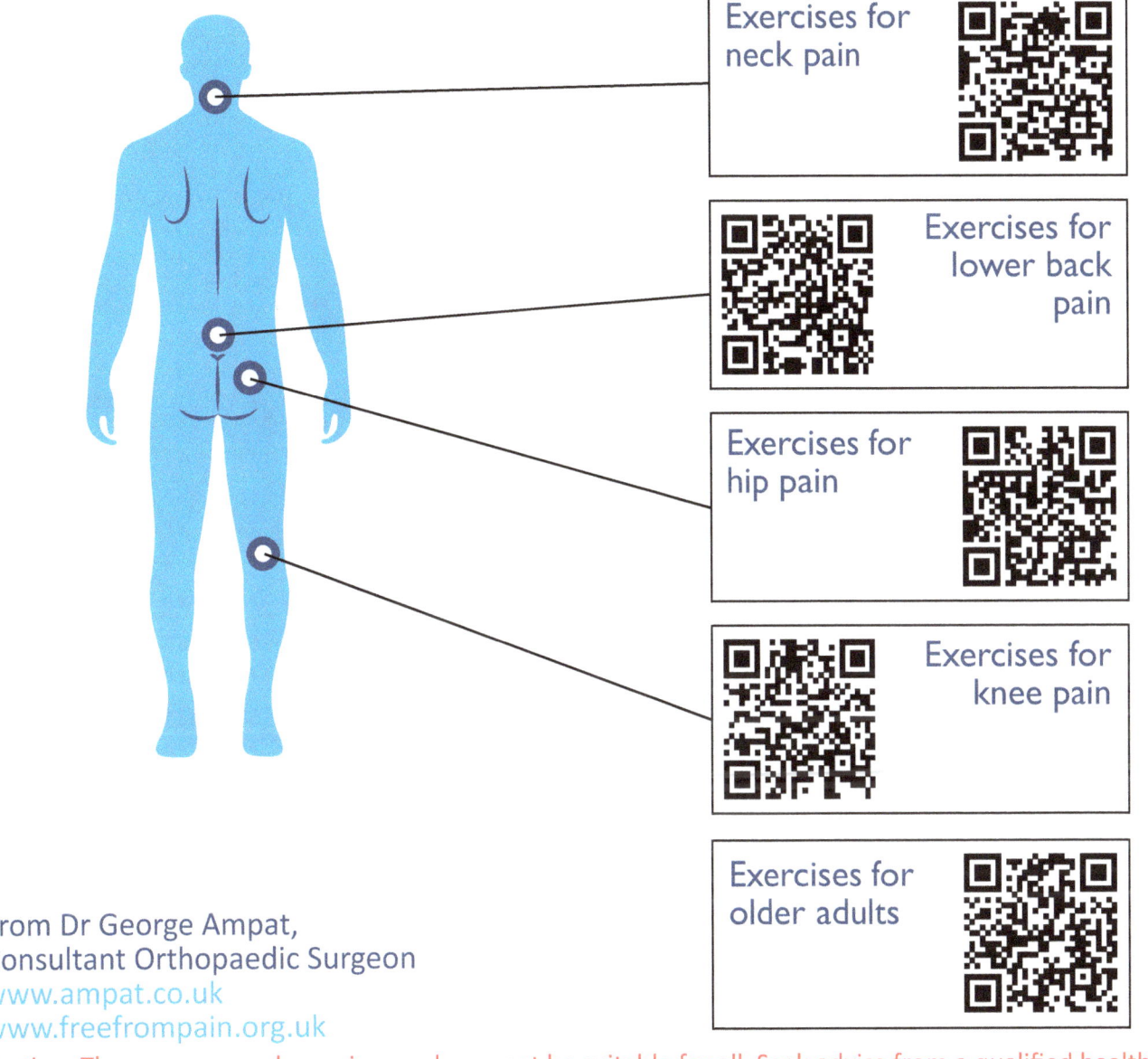